THE RISE & FALL
OF RAJNEESHPURAM

THE RISE & FALL
OF RAJNEESHPURAM

An Historical
Commentary By

Sven Davisson

REBEL SATORI PRESS
New Orleans & New York

Published in the United States of America by
Rebel Satori Press
www.rebelsatoripress.com

The views expressed in these essays are those of the author and do not necessarily reflect the views of the publisher. The information provided in these essays is for general informational purposes only and should not be construed as professional advice. Readers should consult with appropriate professionals for specific advice related to their individual situations. The publisher and the author make no representations or warranties with respect to the accuracy or completeness of the contents of this work and specifically disclaim all warranties, including without limitation warranties of fitness for a particular purpose.

Portions of this book appeared in *Ashé Journal*, 2003.
Photographs by Rob Crandall, licensed through Alamy; except as noted.

Paperback ISBN: 978-1-60864-197-0

I GO TO THE FEET
OF THE AWAKENED ONE

I GO TO THE FEET
OF THE COMMUNE
OF THE AWAKENED ONE

I GO TO THE FEET
OF THE ULTIMATE TRUTH
OF THE AWAKENED ONE

I GO TO THE FEET
OF THE AWAKENED ONE

I GO TO THE FEET
OF THE COMMUNE
OF THE AWAKENED ONE

I GO TO THE FEET
OF THE ULTIMATE TRUTH
OF THE AWAKENED ONE

Chapter One
Beginnings

The Bhagwan Shree Rajneesh (later known simply as Osho) was born Chandra Mohan on December 11, 1931, in Kuchwada, Madhya Pradesh, India. Due to the young boy's grace, his family began calling him "raja" or "king" at an early age. By his own account, he attained the state enlightenment on March 21, 1953, though he kept it a secret for many years after. He taught briefly at a Sanskrit university and began traveling the country teaching.

In the 1960s, Osho began to attract a following in India and started giving lectures on spirituality and meditation. He gained popularity for his unconventional approach to spirituality and his emphasis on the importance of living in the present moment. In 1964, he conducted large meditation camps at locations such as Mt. Abu. In 1970, Rajneesh settled in Bombay, where he began to give regular discourses to a growing number.

In Bombay, Rajneesh initiated his first disciples, giving his twist on the ancient Indian tradition of sannyasa. He called his new descipleship neo-sannyas. This too caused much controversy as the initiatory tradition is deeply rooted in Indian culture. It is generally characterized by a renunciation of the

Facing: Participants in Dynamic Meditation, Rajneeshpuram, 1982
Preceding: The road to Rajneeshpuram

worldly. In Rajneesh's world, it meant the exact opposite. He described the path of the sannyasin as being a Buddha within the world.

In 1974, the movement, under the management of Ma Laxmi, bought land in the Indian town of Pune, north of Mumbai (Bombay). Laxmi was the first in a line of powerful female "personal secretaries" who would hold despotic control over the religious movement's business. Rajneesh and his early disciples moved to the Pune compound in the Koregaon Park neighborhood and established the Acharya Rajneesh Ashram.

At the ashram, Rajneesh gave daily morning discourses (alternating Hindi and English) and held evening meetings and darshans, where he initiated new disciples and answered personal questions. Throughout the 1970s, the ashram attracted increasing international visitors and became one of the focal points of spiritual tourism, which flourished throughout the decade.

Rajneeh's talks covered the entire religious spectrum—from Indian teachers to Jewish mystics to the wisdom of Zen Masters. He introduced several revolutionary "active" meditation techniques designed specifically for the Western mind, combining exorcism and mindfulness. In addition to various meditations, many therapy techniques and workshops arose at the ashram. By the late 1970s, the "therapists" had become something akin to a priestly class within the movement. Osho emphasized the importance of individual freedom and encouraged his followers to question authority and traditional religious teachings.

Osho's, née Bhagwan Shree Rajneesh, core belief was that

individuals should be free to explore their spirituality without the constraints of traditional religious dogma. He encouraged his followers to question authority and to seek their path to enlightenment.

Osho also often spoke about the importance of living in the present moment rather than dwelling on the past or worrying about the future. He taught that true happiness could only be found by embracing the present and letting go of attachments to material possessions and societal expectations.

Osho taught that there were two paths to enlightenment: the path of meditation and the path of love. He emphasized meditation in the traditional Zen style and an active variety of his design called Dynamic Meditation. The latter, he said, was more appropriate for the Western mind, which was less accustomed to sitting silently. He believed that through meditation, individuals could achieve inner peace and transcendence and ultimately understand their true nature. By cultivating a state of mindfulness, individuals can break free from the chains of mental conditioning, anxiety, and desires, ultimately achieving a state of pure consciousness. In contrast, he taught that some individuals were more suited to a path of devotional love in their journey to the divine.

At the heart of Osho's teachings lies the transformative power of self-awareness and meditation. His dynamic Meditation, a dynamic sequence of breathing exercises, cathartic movements, and periods of silence, is a powerful tool designed to shatter the layers of conditioning, leading to heightened awareness and a profound connection with one's inner self.

Osho advocated for the harmonious integration of

spirituality and materialism. He coined the term "Zorba the Buddha," symbolizing the synthesis of the ordinary, pleasure-seeking aspects of life (Zorba) with the spiritual, meditative dimensions (Buddha). According to Rajneesh, one could fully engage in the material world while simultaneously experiencing spiritual transcendence. This perspective challenges the traditional dichotomy between worldly pursuits and spiritual enlightenment.

From the start, Osho's teachings were controversial and often criticized by traditional religious and political leaders. He was accused of promoting a cult-like atmosphere among his followers, and there were allegations of sexual misconduct and drug use within his community. Osho was also critical of many traditional religious practices, leading to criticism from religious leaders worldwide.

Osho's philosophy offers a unique perspective on the nature of the self. He believed that the self is not a fixed entity but a constantly evolving process. Osho taught that the self is not something to be found but something to be created through conscious awareness and self-exploration. His teachings invite individuals to embrace their true nature, free from societal expectations or traditional religious teachings.

Rajneeshpuram was a community established in the early 1980s by followers of the Indian guru Bhagwan Shree Rajneesh, later known as Osho. The community, located in rural Oregon, was intended to be a utopian society based on his teachings. Rajneeshpuram was located in Wasco County, Oregon, on a vast tract of land known as the Big Muddy Ranch, which was initially a cattle ranch in cattle ranch country. The site was chosen for its remote and rural location, providing an ideal setting for establishing the utopian community that Rajneesh and his followers envisioned. The transformation of the former cattle ranch into Rajneeshpuram represented a significant departure from its original purpose and marked a unique chapter in the history of the Oregon countryside.

The development of Rajneeshpuram quickly became controversial as the community began clashing with local residents and government authorities. The movement's outspoken leader, Ma Anand Sheela, became a lightning rod for prejudice. Tensions rose as the community grew in size and influence, leading to conflicts over land use, zoning laws, and political power.

In 1984, the situation escalated when Rajneeshpuram leaders were implicated in a bioterror attack, poisoning salad bars in restaurants in The Dalles, Oregon. This event, known as the Rajneesh bioterror attack, led to a massive investigation and the eventual collapse of the Rajneeshpuram community.

Following the investigation and legal battles, Bhagwan Shree Rajneesh was deported from the United States, and the Rajneeshpuram compound was eventually disbanded and the land sold. Decades later, Rajneeshpuram and the nearby ghost town of Antelope (for a short time, Rajneesh) were becoming a footnote to history. Then came the hit Netflix limited series *Wild Wild Country*. The series presented a captivating exploration of the controversial rise and fall of the Rajneeshpuram community. The series delves into the fascinating and often contentious events surrounding the group's arrival, their conflicts with the local community, and the confrontation between xenophobia and a unique utopian experiment.

Rajneeshpuram witnessed significant infrastructure developments during its short existence. Under Sheela's direction, the sannyasins turned an unremarkable cattle ranch into a city capable of sustaining thousands. At its height, the city maintained a municipality capable of supporting a peak population of 7,000.

The community invested in creating a robust infrastructure, including building a dam and reservoir, a fire department, and a school. The construction of a sewage system, roads, and housing units also reflected the community's commitment to creating a self-sufficient and well-organized settlement. These infrastructure developments were part of Rajneeshpuram's ambitious vision to create a thriving and sustainable commune in the Oregon countryside.

To provide water for the growing number of residents, they created a reservoir known as Krishnamurti Lake. The 80-foot damn created a body of water that covered 45 acres, with a capacity of 330,000,000 gallons. For creek restoration and erosion control, one million willow trees were planted along the creeks, which would both hold the soil and retain some water for the whole ecosystem, and two hundred check dams were built.

The US Postal Service issued the zip code 97741 to the incorporated municipality of Rajneeshpuram.

The Big Muddy Ranch Airport was established by the community to transport supplies and passengers to Rajneeshpuram. To transport cargo and passengers, the

Rajneeshees formed an airline called Air Rajneesh, which operated large commuter aircraft out of Big Muddy Ranch Airport. The airline ferried sannyasins from Portland to the ranch. It consisted of five planes, including a 1948 19-passenger Convair CV-240, two Douglas C-47 Skytrains, a 10-passenger Britten-Norman BN-2 Islander, and even a helicopter.

Of course, Rajneesh was most known for his fleet of luxury cars. The contemporary press dubbed him "the Rolls-Royce Guru." Though the reported numbers of cars owned differ, the most common number quoted is 93. In an article published in the Summer 2015 edition of *The Spirit* magazine, Marinus Rijkers tracked down and verified ownership of 86 cars. Many of the cars received distinctive custom paint jobs by Swami Deva Peter, who published a photo book entitled *93 Rolls-*

Royces.

The Rajneesh organization took delivery of the first Rolls-Royce while still in India. A white 1979 Silver Wraith II arrived at the ashram in November of that model year. Soon after he arrived in the United States while staying at the meditation center in New Jersey, the master himself purchased a Rolls-Royce. In *Don't Kill Him*, Sheela recalls their first drive the next day:

To drive with Bhagwan, even in a brand new Rolls-Royce, was like giving an open invitation to death. He became a beast behind the wheel. To Him traffic signs were just decorations on the streets. Other drivers used their vehicles for transportation purposes; He rode for fun. As usual, that day too He raced like a madman.

Though she does not note the model, it was likely a Camargue. Rijkers notes in his article that the movement is thought to have owned four, though he could only track down three.

Rajneesh had a strong preference for the Silver Spur. This model, a long-wheel-based version of the Silver Spirit, accounted for all but six of the cars Rijkers documents. In interviews in *The Last Testament*, Rajneesh commented that the model "suited him" and noted that the seat was exceptionally comfortable for his problematic back.

The media was fascinated by the cars. When he began giving media interviews in the mid-eighties, Rajneesh was often asked about them. He spoke of the cars as a means of attacting attention to the commune:

It is for those idiots that I am keeping all those Rolls Royces,

*because they cannot move their eyes away from those Rolls Royces. And meanwhile I will go on pouring other things in their minds. Without those Rolls Royces they would not have asked a single question. Those Rolls Royces are doing their work. Every idiot around the world is interested in them. And I want them to be somehow interested -- in anything in Rajneeshpuram. Then we will manage about other things. (*The Last Testament, Vol. 4*)*

During a series of discourses given in the spring of 1986, Osho described the car collection, and the Oregon experiment itself, as a device to poke at Western materialism:

Those cars fulfilled their purpose. They created jealousy in the whole of America, in all the super-rich people. If they were intelligent enough, then rather than being my enemies they would have come

9

*to me to find a way to get rid of their jealousy, because it is their problem. Jealousy is a fire that burns you, and burns you badly. You are in the hands of somebody else. (*Beyond Pyschology*)*

It seems that in India, talking about sex and spirituality was highly controversial. After arriving in the United States, he needed a new means of jabbing at the underpinnings of cultural preconceptions.

At the liquidation of the commune's assets, Texas car dealer Bob Roethlisberger purchased 85 of the cars for $7M.

From the City of Rajneeshpuram comprehensive plan a three volume, 663 page, highly detailed technical plan for the city's development produced in 1982.

Chapter Two
Seeing Red in Cattle Country

In 1981, another female disciple, Ma Anand Sheela, displaced Laxmi as Bhagwan's secretary. Under Sheela's direction, they searched for land large enough to establish a commune. Laxmi was banished from the ashram and sent out to search for possible sites in India. Meanwhile, Sheela funneled several million dollars to a small New Jersey meditation center, Chidvilas. Later that year, Rajneesh flew to the United States on a medical visa granted under the pretext that he was to receive treatment for his back. The group remained in New Jersey for a few months and then moved to Oregon, where Sheela had purchased a defunct ranch known locally as "the Big Muddy." The ranch comprised 64,000 acres (126 square miles) of Oregon desert land and few buildings. Though Sheela presented herself as a shrewd businessperson, she paid $5.75 million for land assessed for the previous year's taxes at only $198,000.

Over the next three years, Rajneesh sannyasins would transform this unpromising parcel into a city that supported at its height 7,000 regular residents with 15,000 annual visitors (mainly concentrated into annual July-August "World Celebrations"). The town, incorporated briefly as Rajneeshpuram, Oregon, had its own post office, school, fire

Rajneeshpuram
The First Annual World Celebration · 1982

in
Central Oregon
July 3 -7

in the presence of
Bhagwan Shree Rajneesh

In the heart of Central Oregon's beautiful mountain scenery lies the 64,229 acre Rajneeshpuram ranch, an exciting adventure in co-operative farming and communal living created by the disciples of Bhagwan Shree Rajneesh. This July, on the occasion of Guru Purnima Day — the traditional eastern celebration when disciples and devotees gather in the presence of the Master — we are holding a religious festival at the ranch in the presence of Bhagwan.

July also marks the first anniversary of Rajneeshpuram's birth. The festival will last for five days, during which morning Satsang will be held daily in Bhagwan's presence, and a special celebration has been arranged for Guru Purnima Day itself (July 6th). The five-day event is open to sannyasins, friends and members of the public. All are welcome.

A full program of meditation and celebration is being offered (details are enclosed) plus periods of extended stay in which people can participate in additional meditation and inner growth programs, or experience commune living — an opportunity to live and work as a member of the ranch community. A temporary meditation hall is being constructed and a small city of tents will be available for accommodation. Recreational activities will be available. We are sure this will be a beautiful and joyful occasion, and we look forward to seeing you here.

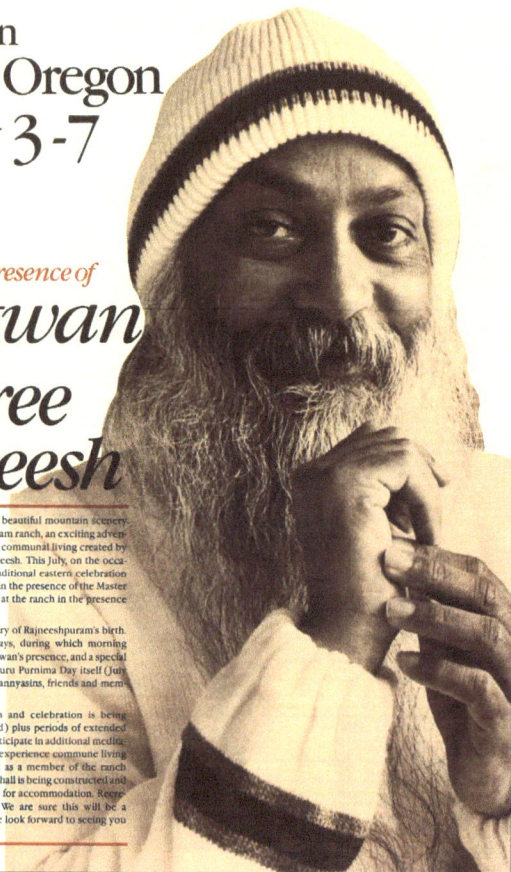

Rajneeshpuram Historical Archives, Pacifc University

and police departments, downtown malls, and restaurants. Its state-of-the-art reservoir even won an award for its innovative ecological design.

Change of this scale, of course, puts stress on the local community. The commune residents, especially the management, were quickly at odds with the nearby town of Antelope. The Attorney General of Oregon, David Frohnmeyer, maintained throughout that the incorporation of Rajneeshpuram violated the constitutional separation of church and state. His action against Rajneeshpuram was still working toward the Oregon Supreme Court in 1985. An "environmental" group, 1,000 Friends of Oregon, also fought the incorporation of Rajneeshpuram from the first public hearing onwards.

Due to the questionable standing of Rajneeshpuram and the objections of 1,000 Friends to commercial use of the Ranch, the Oregon Land Use Commission suggested that the sannyasins locate their publishing and distribution business in the closest town, Antelope. The commune began to purchase real estate in the city, and sannyasins registered to vote. Before sannyasins relocated there, the population of Antelope, OR, was 40, primarily elderly and retired. Due to the influx of new residents, three sannyasins were elected to the six-person town council. The three older councilors refused to sit in the same room with the newly elected sannyasins and effectively resigned their seats. Through default, the Rajneesh followers took over the city government. Around this time, the 40 original Antelope residents unsuccessfully attempted to disincorporate the town.

A similar chain of events occurred with the town school board. At the resident's request, the sannyasins agreed to educate their children at Rajneeshpuram, not Antelope schools. The school tax the residents of Rajneeshpuram paid, however, continued to support the Antelope school. Sannyasins were then elected to the Antelope school board. The previous board had gerrymandered the school district to keep Rajneeshpuram outside its boundaries. The county invalidated the election of the non-sannyasin board members because, in redrawing the district, they had mistakenly drawn their own homes outside the new district. Not residing in the school district, they were no longer eligible to be on the board. Again, the sannyasins "took over" by default.

These occurrences and the sannyasin purchase of real estate in Antelope—the mayor herself working as a real estate agent for most transactions—were used against the Rajneesh sannyasins. Attorney General Frohnmeyer, state congressmen, state senators Hatfield and Packwood, as well as the "concerned citizens" of Oregon, viewed these actions as a take-over and argued that the aggressive sannyasins would not stop short of attempting to take over the county and then the state. The sannyasin presence was quickly characterized as threatening eastern Oregon's way of life. Sannyasin's control of Antelope was seen as a coup de tat, not a democratic process at work. For many government players, taking over the school board was the moment the tide turned entirely against the commune and its residents.

Throughout this period, Rajneesh himself was entirely silent. When he came to America, he had entered a silent period—never speaking publicly. Instead, he said, teaching through his presence. As the Oregon battle began to hit the national media, first appearing on an episode of ABC's Nightline in 1983, the U.S. immigration service began arguing the invalidity of Rajneesh's visa. His medical visa had been renewed as a teaching visa, and the authorities asserted that one could not be a teacher if one did not teach, i.e., talk publicly. Ironically, at the same time, Oregon's Attorney General was arguing that Rajneesh and his followers were a religion and, as such, were violating the constitutional separation of church and state.

Rajneeshpuram exemplifies both the best and the worst of a modern cult phenomenon. The collective activity of the commune residents gave rise to the greatest intentional community experiment the contemporary age has seen. In an article in *The New Yorker*, journalist Frances Fitzgerald detailed some of the accomplishments the commune had managed by 1983: cleared and planted 3,000 acres of land, built a 350-million-gallon reservoir and 14 irrigation systems, created a truck farm that provided 90% of the vegetables needed to feed that Ranch, a poultry and dairy farm to provide milk and eggs, a 10-megawatt power substation, an 85-bus public transportation system, an urban-use sewer system, a state-of-the-art telephone and computer communications center and 250,000 sq. feet of residential space.

Conversely, the commune was a complex business structure built to centralize absolute power in one person, Ma Anand Sheela. She and her band of loyal supporters ran the commune with a hefty hand and provided a combative public face that the media readily and appreciatively displayed. By 1985, there was increased hardship and unrest within the commune itself. Sheela and her coterie of female managers, known collectively as the "Mas," created what Rajneesh himself would later refer to as "a fascist concentration camp." Upon entering the U.S., Sheela established the religion of Rajneeshism, created a bible in the three-volume Book of Rajneeshism, and began to style herself as a high priestess. By 1984, she had started wearing "papal" style robes. Bhagwan's silence lent de facto support to the transformation of Sheela's movement.

Without question, that power corrupted Sheela. She described herself as Queen (and Rajneesh was her king) and started to speak of sannyasins as "her people." She relished confrontation and pursued rather than backed down from a fight—whether with the media, local officials, INS inspector, or a fellow sannyasin. When she spoke, it was taken as if Rajneesh spoke. She was the Metatron speaking for the silent, remote godhead.

During the later period of Rajneeshpuram, tension arose between Jesus Grove, Sheela's compound, and Lao Tzu House, Rajneesh's residence. In late 1984, Rajneesh began speaking again to small groups of sannyasins invited into his house. When Rajneesh informed Sheela he would start speaking, witnesses said she begged him not to. When he finally did begin talking publicly again, Sheela spent days in her room crying. Rajneesh's talks were videotaped and later played to the whole commune. During the summer of 1984, Sheela attempted to cancel the public display of the talks, claiming they were interfering with building the commune. A minor rebellion erupted, and she relented, allowing the videos to be shown late at night when few of the exhausted sannyasins could stay awake to view them.

Satya Bharti's book Promises of Paradise describes one night when the video was not shown. Sheela announced that the tape had been accidentally destroyed. In this talk called "Number 20," Bhagwan spoke out against Sheela and her management of the commune, saying that she had transformed paradise into a "fascist concentration camp." He also outlined his concept of a world filled with autonomous communes where no person would have absolute power.

Ma Nirgun (Rosemary Hamilton), Rajneesh's cook during the later commune period, relates her experiences living in Lao Tzu House in Hellbent for Enlightenment. Under the pretext of security, Sheela ordered the construction of a large fence, complete with guard towers, around Rajneesh's residence. Guards armed with Uzi's followed Rajneesh and his entourage everywhere. No one entered or left Lao Tzu without Sheela knowing about it. Nirgun tells of one day walking outside the house and realizing that the fence was not to keep attackers out but to keep the residents in. "When I got back to Lao Tzu, I suddenly saw it with new eyes: a prison. The high link fence, the gates that delivered a powerful shock, the guardhouse towering over us, manned round the clock by two still figures holding guns—until this moment, I had seen them as a deterrent to hostile outsiders. Now, they seemed to be directed against us." She also talks about a conversation with one of the sentries, a sannyasin who had previously been her friend. She asked why the sannyasin's attitude toward her had grown cold and distant. He replied, "Sheela's orders." Nirgun asked if Sheela had explained her order. "She says it isn't good to get friendly with people you might have to shoot."

During this time, Rajneesh issued lists of "enlightened" sannyasins. These lists were interesting for the people they excluded rather than included. Sheela and her group were conspicuously absent. I feel that Rajneesh was using these lists to destabilize Sheela's power, which ultimately rested on her connection to the guru. Simultaneously, his physician, Amrito, and Ma Prem Hasya developed a relationship. The latter was a member of a wealthy clique of Hollywood-connected sannyasins. This way, Rajneesh connected with an alternative to Sheela's management team.

In September 1985, Sheela and a small group of core supporters abruptly left the commune for Europe. On the day of her departure, Rajneesh held a press conference where he accused Sheela of stealing millions of dollars and attempting to murder him, several sannyasins, and local politicians. He publicly repudiated Rajneeshism and his role as the guru. "I don't give them any commandments," Rajneesh said in a July 17, 1985 interview with *Good Morning America*. "I insistently emphasize that they are not my followers but only fellow travelers." He also called on the FBI to conduct an independent investigation. The FBI quickly found an extensive eavesdropping system wired throughout the commune residences, public buildings, offices, and even Rajneesh's bedroom. Authorities also uncovered a secret lab where, according to later testimony, Ma Puja, the commune nurse referred to by some as "nurse Mengale," had run a poison lab experimenting with biotoxins—including HIV and salmonella.

It was later revealed in court testimony that Sheela's group had attempted to poison two local communities by dumping salmonella into salad bars of several local restaurants. According to a report published in the Journal of the American Medical Association, the actual cause of the mysterious outbreaks would never have been discovered if not for the testimony of conspirators. Salmonella sample disks found at Rajneeshpuram were subsequently matched to the strain of bacteria isolated from the salad bars. This episode has the unfortunate distinction of being the first instance of modern bioterrorism in the U.S. Sheela's group also allegedly fire-bombed a county records office in The Dalles. One of the charges most heavily investigated was the poisoning of Swami Deveraj (later Amrito), Bhagwan's physician. After the July 6 discourse, Ma Shanti Bhadra hugged Deveraj and jabbed him with a needle. The syringe contained a still unidentified poison concocted by Rajneeshpuram nurse Ma Puja. Deveraj became gravely ill and almost died at the Madras hospital.

By October 1985, Rajneesh was on a private plane headed across the country accompanied by his physician Amrito and new secretary Hasya. The aircraft was seized while refueling in Charlottesville, North Carolina, and all on board were arrested. This began a long process of returning him to Oregon to face immigration charges for allegedly arranging sham marriages. Federal agents opted to take a circuitous route across the country rather than flying direct.

Within a month, Rajneesh was again on a plane headed out

of the country, having entered an Alford plea to two counts of immigration fraud. He briefly returned to India and then went on to Kathmandu. This began what his followers term his "world tour," which included refusals from more than 17 countries and forcible deportations from Greece and Uruguay. He and his followers maintained that the countries' resistance to allowing his entrance was due to secret, behind-the-scenes pressure from the Reagan administration—a charge not entirely lacking in credibility.

By the end of the Oregon experiment, 25 sannyasins were charged with electronic eavesdropping conspiracy, 13 immigration conspiracy, eight lying to federal officials, three harboring a fugitive, three criminal conspiracy, one burglary, one racketeering (RICO), one first-degree arson, two second-degree assault, three first degree assault, and three attempted murder. A complex series of plea bargains followed. Sheela was fined $400,000 and ordered to pay $69,353 in restitution. She was sentenced to concurrent prison terms of 20 years for the attempted murder of Sw. Deveraj, 20 years for first-degree assault in the poisoning of county commissioner William Hulse, 10 years for second-degree assault in the poisoning of commissioner Raymond Matthew, four years for the salmonella poisoning, four for wiretapping, and five years probation for immigration fraud. She served only two years in a federal medium security prison and was released for good behavior in December 1988.

Ma Puja also received concurrent sentences: 15 years for the Deveraj murder attempt, 15 for the Hulse poisoning, seven for the Matthew poisoning, four for her role in salmonella poisonings, and three years probation for wiretapping conspiracy. Puja also served only 2 years of her sentence. Like Sheela, she served her sentence at the federal prison in Pleasanton, CA, and was released in December 1988. Rajneesh was charged with one count of criminal conspiracy (RICO) and 34 counts of making false statements to federal officials (INS officers). He entered his plea on two counts of immigration fraud and agreed to pay a $400,000 fine. He was given a 10-year suspended sentence and ordered to leave the country and not return for a minimum of 5 years. Rajneesh corporations agreed to drop all appeals to the ruling that Rajneeshpuram's incorporation was unconstitutional, abandon all claims to the money and jewels impounded in North Carolina, pay $400,000 to the State of Oregon in compensation for investigative costs, $500,000 to settle the claims of four restaurants who suffered losses due to the poisonings, an additional $400,000 to the restaurant owners, $5 million to the Oregon state victim's fund and to sell the ranch. In exchange, Dave Frohnmeyer agreed to drop all RICO charges against the corporations. (Carter, pp. 236-238)

Sannyasins in India finally settled with the Indian government concerning back taxes on the Pune ashram, and Rajneesh returned to his homeland. Through the late 1980's, Rajneesh dropped off the spiritual radar. He dropped the title Bhagwan and, later, even the name Rajneesh. His followers began calling him simply Osho, a Japanese honorific used when referring to a Zen master.

Aerial photograph of central Rajneeshpuram looking northwest, part of a collection of survelience images taken on behalf of the Oregon State Police and found in the files of Bob Oliver, then Governor Victor Atiyeh's legal counsel. (Rajneeshpuram Historical Archive, Pacific University)

Chapter Three
Better Dead Than Red

In four years, the followers of the Bhagwan Shree Rajneesh did what no one thought they could. They raised a city from the desert. They established an almost entirely self-sufficient community of several thousand on land capable of supporting only nine head of cattle. Forty years later, it is evident that the episode of Rajneeshpuram also stands for other things. The events of 1981-1985 expose the pervasiveness of American xenophobia and the potential for the American legislative and judicial systems to be used by a few, with the backing of the masses, to destroy a foreign, unfamiliar minority.

Even before coming to the United States, Rajneesh was on the radar screens of the U.S. State Department. After the murders and mass suicide at Jonestown, the U.S. government began to monitor gurus and religious groups that attracted a large American following. In the late 70's, CIA agents were often rumored to be among the visitors at the Rajneesh ashram. At the very least, the American consulate in Bombay sent reports to Washington regarding the activities of Rajneesh and his Pune ashram. Those reports contained specific references to State Department concerns that Rajneesh would try to relocate to the United States.

In 1981, Rajneesh and a small selection of sannyasins rented a commercial airliner's entire first-class section and flew to New

Jersey. Notable for her absence was Ma Laxmi, who had been left behind in India with a directive to look for land suitable for building a large commune. When Rajneesh traveled to the U.S., everything pointed to his visit being temporary and related to the medical concerns that had provided the reason for his visa. Ma Anand Sheela appeared to be the only person working to make Rajneesh's stay permanent. Soon after the group arrived at the New Jersey meditation center, the recently purchased "castle," Sheela set off to find land for a commune in North America.

When Rajneesh first stepped foot on American soil, he was a "concern" for the U.S. government. By 1984, 17 different local, state, and federal agencies were actively investigating the activities at Rajneeshpuram. White House documents show that Edwin Meese III, the "shadow president" of the Reagan administration, noticed the Rajneesh "situation" as early as 1982. The presence of the Rajneesh commune almost immediately created fear among the local Oregonians—especially the few remaining residents of Antelope. Destruction of the commune became a crusade for Oregon Attorney General David Frohnmeyer and the private activist group 1,000 Friends of Oregon (coincidentally founded by the Attorney General's brother). In a 1984 interview in The Oregonian, Congressman Bob Smith stated he had begun "pounding" the INS to resolve the Oregon-Rajneesh "issue" in April 1982.

As the old saying goes, Just because you are paranoid does not mean they aren't out to get you.

From very early on, Rajneeshpuram was tied up in a

constant barrage of litigation. 1,000 Friends filed numerous lawsuits against the Attorney General's office and private citizens. In April 1983, a horse owned by Harry Hawkins, a former Jefferson County sheriff who had been hired as Rajneeshpuram's first police officer, was killed by buckshot. On July 29, 1983, three bombs exploded at a Rajneesh-owned hotel in Portland.

Oregonians began wearing T-shirts with a picture of the Bhagwan driving a Rolls Royce caught in the cross-hairs of a riflescope while another shirt read "Not Wanted Dead Or Alive." The bumper sticker "Better Dead than Red" became common throughout eastern Oregon. In 1985, several attempts were made to enact legislation that specifically attacked the legitimacy of Rajneeshpuram and sannyasin activity. The Oregon Secretary of State authored a ballot question, wording approved by Attorney General Frohnmeyer, that read, "Shall City of Rajneesh (Antelope) charter be repealed, city cease to exist, and Wasco County assume city's assets and liabilities?" (*The Bend Bulletin*, July 3, 1985)

One of the most persistent myths of Rajneeshpuram over the years following its dissolution is the assumption that the commune blew apart from the inside. This notion that the commune disintegrated due to internal fractures and tensions fits snugly within the popular conception that cults are inherently fleeting, frenetic, fluid, and unstable. The commune suffered unremitting and coordinated harassment from the local, state, and federal governments. This resentment and distrust in the local communities created extreme pressure on Rajneeshpuram and its residents.

Sheela's tactics and combativeness rose in direct proportion to the pressure exerted on the commune from outside. Her increasingly ludicrous reactions were generally the result of new attacks from authorities. Her stranglehold on control of the commune also increased these external forces. These threats also, ironically, became an element of her power, providing the essential component of us-against-them paranoia necessary for the success of an absolutist regime. This was only exacerbated when Rajneesh began speaking again in 1984—a fact which immediately started to work against Sheela's power base.

Rumors and myths about the strangers in red began immediately after they arrived at the Big Muddy. The commune was spending tremendous sums of money on development and the creation of city infrastructure. This seemingly limitless supply of ready cash convinced federal law enforcement officials that the money stemmed from illegal activity such as drug smuggling, gun running, or both. The cash came from many lucrative and highly successful business ventures abroad. Sannyasins operated almost half the vegetarian restaurants in Germany, and Rajneesh discotheques were springing up across Europe. These businesses and the growing number of meditation centers and local communes sent millions of dollars to support Rajneeshpuram.

Another persistent rumor of illegal activity at Rajneeshpuram remains that the sannyasins were stockpiling weapons. Media reports of the day often focused on images of Uzi toting sannyasins. By 1985, Sheela was always shown wearing a gun on her hip. The reports failed to mention that the photographed sannyasins were members of the Rajneeshpuram police force—a state-recognized law enforcement agency whose members had been trained at the State Police Academy. Sheela and other sannyasin spokespeople, such as Mayor Krishna Devi, did nothing to dispel these rumors. Instead, through 1984 and into 1985, they stepped up the rhetoric and counter-threats. Newspapers quoted Devi as warning that they would take 15 Oregonian heads for every sannyasin killed. Sheela repeatedly asserted that the residents of Rajneeshpuram were ready to defend themselves—the use of the words "war" and "blood" every day.

When federal agents searched Rajneeshpuram after the Bhagwan's departure, no stockpile of weapons was discovered. Divers from the Navy Seals were brought in to search the two lakes at Rajneeshpuram. Media reports of the searches failed to mention that no cache of weapons was present. According to subsequent reports, the Rajneesh sannyasins did not possess any guns inconsistent with a municipal police force.

In his book *Passage to America*, Max Brecher interviews two soldiers-for-hire who allege that they were offered money for killing Rajneesh. In both instances, the individuals were sure the CIA was ultimately behind the payment offers. John Wayne Hearn, now serving three life sentences for three gruesome murders for hire, admits to working for the CIA on several covert operations, including running guns to Nicaragua and assisting in a plot to overthrow the government of French Guyana. Hearn claims to have been offered significant money to blow up several trailers at Rajneehpuram to scare the sannyasins. The second man, Don Stewart, recorded his conversations with his contact, Wolfgang. In these conversations, Wolfgang specifically mentions government agencies targeting Rajneesh. Wolfgang planned to assassinate the Bhagwan during one of his daily drives. Once a day, Rajneesh would drive his car along a commune road, and sannyasins would line up to watch their guru drive by. For Wolfgang and presumably his backers, the killing of a couple of hundred devotees was more than acceptable if Rajneesh was taken out. Ironically, the soldiers turned down the offer in both instances due to the rumors they had heard about the commune being an armed camp. The prospect of being trapped by a few thousand armed zealots proved an unacceptable risk.

Under the guise of fighting terrorism, the President authorized the CIA to investigate foreign entities on U.S. soil, thus sidestepping the congressional mandate against domestic CIA operations. In December 1981, President Reagan signed Executive Order 12333, which authorized federal law enforcement agencies to hire outside people to conduct illegal break-ins to obtain evidence. The executive order specifically allowed that evidence thus collected could be used to get a legitimate search warrant.

Beginning in 1983 and increasing to the commune's dissolution in 1985, military jets from Whidbey Island Naval Base conducted regular flyovers of Rajneeshpuram. In violation of FAA regulations, the planes routinely flew extremely low over the commune, disrupting daily life and, in several instances, jeopardizing civilian air traffic at the Rajneesh airport. These flights were ostensibly routine training missions—at times, even using the commune buildings as fake targets for bombing runs. The flights also included reconnaissance and surveillance. Twin-engine Mohawk surveillance planes from the reconnaissance unit in Boise, Idaho, also conducted recons over the commune. In the taped conversations with Wolfgang, he mentions participating in aerial surveillance. Both the INS and U.S. attorney's office conducted aerial recons over Rajneeshpuram in 1985 as part of their preparation for arresting Rajneesh.

On May 13, 1985, the police of Philadelphia, PA, dropped a C-4 bomb onto the headquarters of M.O.V.E., a back-to-Africa movement. The police had attempted to serve warrants on members of the movement, and they were allegedly fired upon during the attempt. After a brief siege, Philadelphia Police Commissioner Gregore Sambor ordered the dropping of a bomb onto the headquarters building—one of several row houses in the Philadelphia residential neighborhood. (*The New York Times*, May 14, 1985) The ensuing fire destroyed 61 row houses, leaving 251 people without a home. (CNN, June 24, 1996) Following the bombing, Commissioner Sambor was reelected, and U.S. Attorney General Edwin Meese III applauded the operation as a superb success for American law enforcement. By 1996, Philadelphia had paid almost $30 million in lawsuits resulting directly from the M.O.V.E. operation.

In the summer of 1985, Sheela retained a top immigration lawyer, Peter Schey, to represent Rajneesh in his ongoing battle with INS. Schey began negotiating with U.S. District Attorney Robert Turner, who had secretly convened a grand jury to investigate alleged immigration fraud at Rajneeshpuram. Schey wanted to ensure that if indictments were handed

Rajneesh and Sheela leaving INS office

down, the indictees would be allowed to surrender themselves to authorities outside of Rajneeshpuram. Schey was confident that he had an agreement with Turner and that Rajneesh and any others indicted would be notified 24 hours in advance and allowed to turn themselves into the courthouse in Portland. Despite this, according to INS deputy counsel Mike Inman, Turner had no intention of allowing Rajneesh or anyone else to surrender peacefully. Instead, in Inman's words, Turner was set on "storming the Bastille." According to Inman, Turner wanted "to utilize the Oregon National Guard, the FBI, and the Immigration Services Border Patrol, and storm the compound with force, and go through the barricades and fences." (Brecher, p. 275) According to Inman and others involved, Turner had planned to serve the warrants unannounced. INS agent Joe Greene testified under oath that Turner had no intention of allowing the Bhagwan to surrender at a neutral location. According to the plan, state and federal law enforcement, including the Bureau of Alcohol, Tobacco, and Firearms, would show up unannounced at Rajneeshpuram and, on a bull-horn inform the residents that they were surrounded and that the indictees had 1 minute to surrender. National Guard troops would be concealed in the nearby hills to provide necessary backup. Given the then generally accepted rumors that the commune was a "militarized camp," this plan would seem to have been intended to provoke an armed confrontation.

The government's plan for Rajneeshpuram eerily foreshadows the later federal assaults on the Branch Davidian compound at Waco, Texas, and Randy Weaver's cabin at Ruby Ridge, Idaho. In these two instances, tactics similar to Turner's were employed with tragic results. In these cases, the fear that stockpiles of weapons were present was used to justify the excessive force employed. Through the period leading up to the arrest of Rajneesh and again during the siege at the Branch Davidian compound, media pundits repeatedly raised the specter of Jonestown. The deaths of the Davidians are still often represented as mass suicide rather than the consequence of the government's assault. It is not difficult to imagine what would have happened if Robert Turner had been able to proceed with his surprise entrance into Rajneeshpuram. One can also assume who would have been accused of "firing first."

Turner's plan was unexpectedly thwarted before it could be implemented when, on the afternoon of Sunday, October 27, 1985, two privately chartered planes departed Rajneeshpuram Airport. They began to make their way across the continent. Rumors were flying that arrests were imminent. In actuality, sealed indictments had been handed to Turner the previous week. Rajneesh's non-sannyasin attorney, Peter Schey, twice flew from Los Angeles to Oregon to discuss the rumored warrants and to arrange for the peaceful surrender of Rajneesh. On both occasions, Turner denied the existence of warrants for Rajneesh or any other sannyasin. Turner claimed that he believed that a peaceful surrender was impossible and that by telling Schey, he would be tipping Rajneesh off and allowing him time to flee. Sheela had departed the commune the month before under a cloud of accusation and suspicion— the Bhagwan, himself, her principal accuser. Even though no indictments had been announced nor warrants served, frantic calls went out to law enforcement agencies across the country to apprehend the "fugitives." The planes landed at a small airport outside Charlotte, North Carolina, for refueling. Agents were waiting, and the Bhagwan and his entourage were arrested without incident. Though they had been warned that the passengers would be heavily armed with automatic weapons and armor-piercing bullets, the agents found only one small handgun on the planes. At Rajneesh's bail hearing the next day, prosecutors could not present an arrest warrant from Oregon. Despite this discrepancy, the judge denied Rajneesh's bail. An unsigned, incomplete Oregonian warrant was later given to the Charlotte court. Oregon court records hold a different arrest warrant; however, it appears to have been forged after the fact and pre-dated.

In a jailhouse TV interview by Ted Koppel aired live on ABC's Nightline, Rajneesh asserted that he was not leaving the country or fleeing impending arrest. When asked by an incredulous Ted Koppel if the Bahamas (their flight plans indicated North Carolina, but sannyasins were reported to have been inquiring about renting a plane capable of over-sea flight) was now part of the United States, Rajneesh claimed not to know where the planes were headed. Instead, he said that he trusted his friends, and all he knew was that they were taking him somewhere safe. Given Rajneesh's apparent lack of involvement in his travel decisions during his post-U.S. "world tour," it is not out of the question that he did not know where the planes were headed. He would go where they were headed like a Zen sage; he was where ever he was.

One thing is sure: Rajneesh's departure from Rajneeshpuram stemmed from the government's plan for a major assault on the commune and, thus, likely spared several hundred lives. By late September 1985, 15 National Guard armored personnel carriers were positioned in the hills surrounding Rajneeshpuram. In addition to the many FBI agents investigating the allegations made by Rajneesh, the state was ready to commit 800 state troopers if conflict erupted, and the National Guard had another 600 guardsmen on standby as backup. By September 30, the National Guard had three HUEY helicopters at Redmond airport ready to carry FBI agents and Oregon State Police SWAT teams into Rajneeshpuram. Turner also unsuccessfully requested U.S.

Marshal's Service Fugitive Investigative Search Teams (FIST) and Border Patrol from the U.S.-Mexico border to assist with "mass arrests."

Even if one rejects his claim that he was not fleeing the country, one question does remain about this mysterious flight: why did they turn east rather than west? If they had chosen to fly out over the Pacific Ocean, they would have quickly been over international waters outside U.S. jurisdiction. *A Passage to America* author Max Brecher asked this question directly to Rajneesh in 1989, "I left for Charlotte," Rajneesh answered, "because for six weeks previously, the National Guard was on standby around the commune, ready to enter the commune. If they had arrested me there, the 5,000 sannyasins would not have tolerated it. There would have been bloodshed. To avoid this, I went to Charlotte. It was to avoid the bloodshed of the sannyasins. There were no sannyasins in Charlotte who would be involved if I was arrested there. And there was a beautiful house in the mountains there for me to stay." (Brecher, p. 289) When Weaver was asked about the government's concern about a bloodbath of innocent sannyasins at Rajneeshpuram if the commune was stormed by force, he simply stated, "It's not the government's job to make those guy's jobs easier."

In retrospect, Rajneesh's cross-country flight did not meet the legal definition of fleeing prosecution, and he and the other passengers could not rightly be considered fugitives. U.S. District Attorney conceded in the Charlotte court that he lacked the evidence to support his claim that Rajneesh and co. were attempting to evade arrest. Despite Turner's contention to the contrary in court, the pilots filed flight plans that listed

Charlotte as their final destination. According to the account of the air traffic controller on duty that night, the pilots did not behave in a fashion consistent with someone who was either nervous or paranoid. Above all else, they could not be called fugitives since no warrant existed for them during their arrests. The following morning, the federal indictment was unsealed, but there is still no evidence that an arrest warrant was issued for Rajneesh or anyone else on the plane. The warrant on file in Oregon, though dated Oct. 28, was not clerked into the courthouse until two weeks after the arrest. The warrant also lists the North Carolina arresting officer, a fact that could not have been known at the time the warrant was supposed to have been issued since Rajneesh was still in Oregon at that time. Despite these facts, Rajneesh's attorneys conceded that a warrant existed without seeing it, and the magistrate denied Rajneesh's bail because he was a flight risk.

A theory proposed by Max Brecher and supported by the account of deputy INS council Inman is that the federal authorities—the INS and the US State Department–wanted Rajneesh to flee the country. Then, they could use the existence of indefinitely active warrants to keep him from ever returning. This plan would have effectively prevented Rajneesh from ever entering the United States again without going through lengthy deportation proceedings and possibly a court ruling in his favor. This would help explain why the INS pulled their support for the U.S. District Attorney's investigation and ordered their field operatives not to assist in the arrest of Rajneesh even though all the charges against him were for immigration violations. Turner takes full credit for the arrest. He and a Charlotte INS agent, working against the directives of his superiors, coordinated the bringing in of the U.S. Marshals and the subsequent arrests. His zeal to prosecute Rajneesh may have thwarted the government's quiet solution to the Rajneesh problem.

On July 13, 1986, a monument was dedicated outside the Wasco County Court House. Beneath the statue of a stately Antelope read the inscription "Dedicated to all who steadfastly and unwaveringly opposed the attempts of the Rajneesh followers to take political control of Wasco County: 1981-1985." Below this, the plaque carries a quote from Irish politician Edmund Burke: "The only thing necessary for the triumph of evil is for good men to do nothing." Above the statue flew a flag that had once flown above the U.S. Capital Building—a gift from Congressman Bob Smith. Were the residents of Rajneeshpuram really "evil," and were the Oregonians really "good"? What is true of erecting monuments is also true of history; the victors erect them. The defeated, almost without exception, go down as villains within the orthodox historical record. Only two members of the commune could rightfully be described as "evil"—Ma Anand Sheela and Ma Puja. A few others committed evil acts.

Studies like the Zimbardo experiment have shown that even red-blooded, all-American college students can commit the most atrocious acts if given absolute power over another. In the experiment designed by Philip Zimbardo, a group of male college student volunteers were randomly separated into two groups—prisoners and guards. The guards were given uniforms and dark glasses; no one could address another by name. A long list of petty prisoner regulations was provided to the guards. The experiment, initially designed to last a fortnight, had to be ended after only one week due to an unexpected level of violence and humiliation inflicted on the prisoners by the guards. In his analysis of the experiment, Zygmunt Bauman observes, "clearly and unambiguously, the orgy of cruelty that took Zimbardo and his colleagues by surprise stemmed from a vicious social arrangement, and not from the viciousness of the participants." (Bauman, p. 167) In a separate study by Stanley Milgram at Yale University, Milgram demonstrated that most humans can harm another if the instruction comes from one the subject holds as an authority figure.

Were all sannyasins indeed "evil"? This is undoubtedly the explicit message of the Antelope monument. When the sannyasins first moved to eastern Oregon, buying land that no one else wanted, they made serious efforts towards creating a positive impression on their neighbors. Sheela regularly held information meetings in 1981, where she presented a pleasant face and attempted to charm the wary Oregonians. The sannyasins went above and beyond in complying with local laws and state land use regulations throughout the creation of their city—a fact that infuriated their opponents in the 1,000 Friends of Oregon and the Oregon Attorney General's office. Their comprehensive plan was even an example for other municipalities to follow. At its outset, the commune developers tried to get along with their neighbors and comply with all U.S. laws. They only moved into the neighboring town of Antelope when pushed by 1,000 Friends lawsuits and at the suggestion of the state Land Use Commission.

When the sannyasins began buying property in Antelope, the town was listed prominently on the list of Oregon ghost towns. The settlement was a stop on the stage coach route. It incorporated as a city in 1901 when its population was at it height. The decrease in demand for sheep and the expansion of the Columbia Southern Railroad into Central Oregon, were contributing factors to the decline in population in Antelope following its incorporation. Population dropped to below 100 by the 1940 census. When the Rajneesh sannyasins arrived in 1981, the population had reached a low of 39.

Throughout the creation of Rajneeshpuram, Sheela's arguments and public appearances became increasingly vitriolic and provocative. Also, through this time, the commune and its residents were the victims of an escalating bombardment of harassment and threats of harm. The threats and intimidation came from multiple directions and were fully supported by several arms of the federal government. Against this opposition and the backdrop of the unwelcoming sagebrush desert, it is incredible that the Rajneesh sannyasins accomplished what they did—creating a sustainable, ecologically friendly city capable of supporting thousands of residents.

The history of the United States began with religious dissent—the Puritans forging a life in the wilderness of New England to escape persecution. It is also a history of repressing religious differences. The same Puritan pilgrims established a cluster of communities ruthlessly intolerant of religious differences—Cotton Mather and the Salem witch trials being but one example extreme among many. Attorney General Frohnmeyer asserted that a city founded by adherents of one particular religion was unconstitutional. If American history is to suggest anything, the opposite would certainly seem to be the case. Religious followers established many U.S. cities to develop areas where they could freely practice their faith. The settling of Utah and the incorporation of Salt Lake City is an obvious example. The anti-cult movement has been an equal and counter-running force within the history of religion in the United States. As so-called "new religious movements" have been every day since before the revolution, anti-cult movements have been equally ubiquitous. It was this strain of intolerance that necessitated the moves that led to the establishment of new cities based on religious communities.

Philip Jenkins argues in his book *Mystics & Messiahs* that anti-cult paranoia has frequently taken hold of the American mass psyche. Phillips notes that the arguments of this reactionary movement were solidly in place by the late 19th century—lurid stereotypes, xenophobia, accusations of mind control, and stories of sexual scandal. All these elements are displayed in the voices of the concerned people speaking out against Rajneeshpuram. "When a modern critic attacks a deviant religious group as a cult," Jenkins writes, "the images evoked are ultimately a mélange of rumors and allegations variously made against Catholics, Masons, Mormons, Shakers, radical evangelicals, and others." (Jenkins, p. 25) He further argues that the concern over cults does not necessarily correlate to actual threats posed by the cult's activities. Jenkins observes that "the level of public concern about cults at any given time is not necessarily based on a rational or objective assessment of the threat posed by these groups, but rather reflects a diverse range of tensions, prejudices, and fears." (Jenkins, p. 20)

Again, one has to ask, were the Rajneesh sannyasins "evil" for attempting to build their City on a Hill? Or were they simply victims of a cyclic resurgence of the pernicious hatred of difference that has run through the darkness of America since its earliest days?

Chapter Four
Death of the Master

In 1989, Bhagwan again stopped talking publicly due to his failing health. His final discourse ended with the last word of the Buddha, *samasati*, "remember that you are all Buddhas." That year, he instructed his followers to build him a new marble bedroom following his detailed design. He spent only a short time in this new space before saying he preferred his old bedroom. In January 1990, Osho passed from his body, instructing his physician to place his favorite socks and hat on him. When asked what they should do with him after he died, he said, "Stick me under the bed and forget about me."

Through the 1990s, Rajneesh, now packaged commercially as Osho, became again a significant figure in the spiritual and New Age landscapes. His ashram in Pune transformed into a meditation resort (complete with an air-conditioned modern hotel and "zennis" courts) is now, once again, a popular destination for Western seekers. His books are again available in U.S. bookstores. The Indian government, once his adversary, now appears to embrace the potential tourist dollars represented by Osho and his resort. The library of the Indian Congress has established a separate Osho collection, an honor only held by one other, Mahatma Gandhi, and the *Times of India* named Osho one of its ten most influential Indians of the 20th century.

The events that comprise the rise and fall of Rajneeshpuram raise many more questions than can be answered in a single introductory article such as this. Rajneesh stated that he wanted everything that happens after a religious teacher dies to occur while he was still alive. He often spoke of the mechanism that led from Buddha to the creation of religion and how that process destroyed the religiousness of the teaching. I think that the Oregon experiment was an attempt by Rajneesh to facilitate this process through the simulated death of his silence and ceding control to Sheela. In this way, he could short-circuit the development of religious orthodoxy and protect his sannyasins, later termed "fellow travelers," from the deadening of meditative/devotional religiousness.

This leaves many more significant questions unaddressed. Most notable is the question of a master's responsibility for his disciples. After Sheela's departure, Rajneesh asked pointedly why the sannyasin residents of Rajneeshpuram had not done anything to stop her.

The facts, lies, and enigma surrounding Rajneeshpuram may permanently obscure the full appreciation of what attracted thousands of people to him. All else aside, Rajneesh's teachings represent a post-modern synthesis neither equaled nor paralleled in the 20th century. The breadth of his knowledge and his deft interpretation of ancient masters is unique. His influence, primarily unacknowledged, has been widespread throughout modern devotional spirituality and New Age movements. Many a Rajneesh therapist and dehypnotherapists have become "famous" gurus or teachers. When one reads in a biographical sketch that the teacher spent years in India studying under an unnamed guru, it is more often than not Rajneesh to whom they refer.

The Pune resort is now run by a group called the Inner Circle, a body designed by Osho before his death. A second group of sannyasins has coalesced around the Delhi meditation center, led by Indian disciples Swami Chaitanya Keerti and Ma Yoga Neelam (Hasya's successor as personal secretary and form Inner Council member). A multitude of issues mark the divide between these two groups over the role of the guru, devotion vs. meditation ("path of love" and "path of meditation"), the copyright of his books and art, the access to his teachings, the management of the commune/resort, etc. The articles collected in this issue reflect voices from across the spectrum of sannyasin experiences centered on the ranch experience and the time that followed.

In the small hours of January 19, 1990, the world received news that the controversial teacher Osho, known more broadly as Bhagwan Shree Rajneesh or simply "the Bhagwan," was dead. For most, the news registered, if it did at all, as a footnote to a story from the decade just closing.

The day started like any other at the Osho International Meditation Resort in Pune, India. People from all over the world gathered to meditate in the peaceful gardens and spaces that were well-known for Osho's teachings. But there was a worry in the air as people heard that Osho was ill. He had been sick for a while, and no one knew what was wrong. Despite all the rumors and questions, Osho stayed quiet and told his followers to live in the present moment.

As the sun set that day, a sad feeling spread through the community. News quickly traveled, and people rushed to where Osho was staying, wanting to be there for his last moments. Inside the house, Osho lay on his bed, surrounded by a very select few of his closest followers.

Outside, many people gathered, showing their grief and respect differently. Some cried while others stood quietly, trying to understand what was happening. But there was also a feeling of peace as if everyone knew that Osho's influence would continue beyond his physical presence.

As the night progressed, the resort became increasingly quiet, with only the sound of the wind breaking the silence. Those present noted that it felt like time had stopped, with everyone there fully present.

Osho's body became still, and he took his last breath.

His doctor appeared before those gathered awaiting news. Amrito announced that Osho had passed. "Just take me to Buddha Hall for ten minutes," Amrito recalled Osho saying, "and then take me to the burning ghats – and put my hat and socks on me before you take my body."

Osho's body was taken almost immediately to the burning ghats for cremation. The speed of this process and questions surrounding the official death certificate have caused ongoing controversy, including open accusations of foul play. In 2017, questions about the circumstances of Osho's death became front-page news in India when Puna doctor Abhay Vaidya published the book Who Killed Osho?

Since his passing, rumors and doubt have circulated about the circumstances surrounding Osho's passing. For some time before that January day in 1990, Osho himself had talked often of his health decline being due to his having been poisoned while in US custody in 1985. He pinpointed the cause as thallium poisoning.

Thallium poisoning is a type of heavy metal poisoning that can occur when a person is exposed to high levels of thallium, either through ingestion, inhalation, or skin contact. Symptoms of thallium poisoning can include hair loss, nausea, vomiting, diarrhea, abdominal pain, headache, confusion, seizures, and even coma in severe cases. Thallium is a highly toxic substance and can cause damage to the nervous system, kidneys, and other organs, which can lead to long-term health problems or even death if left untreated. Treatment for thallium poisoning typically involves removing the source of exposure, administering medications to bind with the thallium and remove it from the body, and providing supportive care to manage symptoms and prevent complications. Osho himself first announced his "poisoning" in 1987 during an interview published in the Osho Times. He outlined the mysterious symptoms he had been experiencing: "no resistance to disease, falling weight without any reason, hair becoming white before age, hair falling out without any reason, tingling sensations in the extremities, loss of appetite, tastelessness, nausea, the bone pain in my right hand."

His self-described symptoms and those spoken of posthumously by his doctor do not readily fit the normal model of exposure to thallium. Though the effects, if left untreated, can cause long-term health problems, symptoms are generally acute and proximal to the exposure. Thallium does have a history of utilization as a poison. It has been called "the poisoner's poison" due to the difficulty in detecting its presence. There was a famous series of poisonings in Australia in the early 1950s. Agatha Christie incorporated thallium poisoning as a method of murder in The Pale Horse, published in 1961.

I propose another cause for Osho's decline in health: chronic B12 deficiency brought on by regular and prolonged exposure to nitrous oxide. Osho was a very happy dental patient. One of the first things he had done to his new home in Oregon was to have dental surgery installed. Regular dental sessions had been a common occurrence before the move to America and appeared to have also continued after his return to India. He dictated three books during the Oregon dental sessions: *Glimpses of a Golden Childhood*, *Books I Have Loved* and *Notes of a Madman*. The ability to engage in extensive dictation undercuts the pretense that these sessions were exclusively for dental care. In her memoir *Osho: Intimate Glimpses*, Ma Deva Anando estimates that Osho underwent at least 115 sessions from May 1988 to September 1989. It would seem entirely likely that the frequency of these dental sessions had more to do with a fondness for nitrous than extreme dental care. I think it safe to say, that Osho's frequent exposure to nitrous could at least in part be classified as recreational.

In Notes of a Madman, Osho says:

Actually oxygen and nitrogen are basic elements of existence. They can be of much use, but for reasons the politicians have been against chemicals of all kinds, all drugs. The very word drug had become dangerous. They are so against drugs because people come to know themselves, politicians lose their power over them, and they love their power. In the Vedas they call it soma, the essence, and since those days until today, all those who have known have recognised, either directly or indirectly, that chemicals can be of immense service to man. Man is chemistry, so is existence. All is chemistry....

Though long considered safer in a controlled clinic environment with proper occupational safeguards in place, the rise of the abuse of nitrous as a "party drug" has demonstrated that misuse can have negative consequences on an individual's health. The frequency of use Anando describes puts Osho's exposure at the high end of recreational nitrous users.(Nabben, van den Brink) Over-exposure to nitrous gas has been shown to cause vitamin B12 deficiency—chronic in frequent users. This results in various symptoms, including subacute combined degeneration of the spinal cord that can cause numbness, muscle weakness, and trouble with coordination. Chronic over-users have also exhibited strange and delusional tendencies.(Sethi, Mullin, Torgovnick, et al.) Additional side-impacts can include anemia, pulmonary issues, emphysema, and pneumomediastinum.(Chiang, Hung, Wang, Lee, Yang; Garakani, Jaffe, Savla, et. al.) These symptoms associated with chronic B12 deficiency align well with the general sense of decline routinely described by Osho and his caretakers.

In his final months, Oso also complained of ear-ringing and high-pitched sounds. In December 1989, he told those assembled for discourse he believed that sinister forces were directing sound weapons against him. Research has shown that N2O usage can cause a significant increase in pressure in the middle ear, which has a notable impact on how the subject perceives the intensity of sounds.(Fabijan, Morris , Murray) This could explain Osho's perception of seemingly unusual sound frequencies. Additionally, his negative interpretation of the origin of the sounds may be symptomatic of a heightened sense of delusion and paranoia.

Given that his body was quickly cremated and the questions surrounding his death certificate, we may never know for certain what precipitated his passing. There are those, including Sheela, who have suggested that Osho either committed suicide or died due to over-medication administered by his doctor(s). No matter the ultimate precipitating cause in January 1990, I think it highly probable that the recreational use of N2O over more than a ten-year period played a significant role in his health issues.

Chapter Five
Her Own Rules?

After the closing of Rajneeshpuram, Ma Anand Sheela faced legal troubles. She was arrested and charged with attempted murder, assault, arson, and wiretapping. She pleaded guilty to some of these charges and served time in prison. After her release, she moved to Switzerland and started a new life there. She later wrote a book about her experiences and continues to have a controversial public presence.

After leaving Rajneeshpuram in 1985, Ma Anand Sheela faced a series of legal and personal challenges. She was implicated in various criminal activities that occurred during her time leading the Rajneesh movement, including the bioterrorism attack and wiretapping.

When Sheela and a few close associates left the ranch, they fled to Europe. She was eventually arrested in Germany in 1986 and extradited to the United States. On July 22, 1986, Sheela pleaded guilty to first-degree assault and conspiracy to commit assault against Hulse, and later to second-degree assault and conspiracy to commit assault against Matthew. She also admitted to setting fire to a county office and wire-tapping at the commune. For these offenses, Sheela was initially sentenced to three consecutive 20-year terms in federal prison, which were later reduced to a total of 4½ years to be served concurrently. Additionally, she was fined $470,000. She was released for good behavior from the Federal prison in Dublin, California in 1988 after serving 29 months.

After her release, Sheela settled in Switzerland. She married a Swiss citizen and fellow sannyasin Urs Birnstielin in 1999. That same year, a Swiss court convicted her of "criminal acts preparatory to the commission of murder" for her involvement in a 1985 plot to kill U.S. federal prosecutor Charles Turner. Although the Swiss government declined to extradite her to the U.S., it agreed to prosecute her in Switzerland. She was found guilty of a similar charge under Swiss law and was sentenced to time already served. She currently owns and operates two nursing homes near Basel.

Her story has been the subject of renewed interest, particularly following the 2018 Netflix documentary series *Wild Wild Country*, which brought her and the Rajneesh movement back into the spotlight. She has also authored two memoirs: *Don't Kill Him!: The Story of My Life With Bhagwan Rajneesh* (2013) and *By My Own Rules: My Story in My Own Words* (2021), as well as an authorized biography, *Nothing to Lose* by Manbeena Sandhu (2020). In the spring of 2021, Netflix released *Searching for Sheela* produced by Karan Johar. The series follows Sheela's first return trip to India after 35 years.

Chapter Six
And The Fight Begins

When Amrito announced Osho's death to the followers assembled in Buddha Hall, he quoted Osho as saying to Jayesh at the end, "I leave you my dream." This was interpreted as Osho's passing control of his work to Sw. Anand Jayesh.

Osho had assembled a group of leading sannyasins he called "the Inner Circle" in April 1989. This was announced in the February 1, 1990 edition of the *Osho Times*:

On April 6 1989, Osho gave instructions for the setting up of a committee to be called "The Inner Circle." The aim of the committee, he said, was to reach unanimous decisions about the continued functioning and expansion of the commune and his work. 'I am tired,' he said, 'and I want to retire.'

Over the next few months, Osho closely observed the committee members. Eventually, he finalized the committee with 21 members selected to represent the commune departments and his work. He emphasized that the inner workings of the committee were to remain secret. He also clarified that the committee should not be involved in spiritual considerations but should focus on the commune's practical problems. Osho emphasized that "The Inner Circle" is a pragmatic and practical way to make decisions, not a club for discussing philosophy.

Osho stated that when a member dies, the remaining members must unanimously choose a new member. He appointed Jayesh as Chairman and Amrito as Vice-Chair.

It was not long after the master's death that tensions became evident within the Inner Circle. A growing fight over how to best preserve his legacy and foster a living movement soon became apparent. The differences seemed to break along racial and cultural lines and, from the start, pit devotion against capitalism.

Many followers and observers have been troubled by this controversy over control of Osho's legacy between Westerners and Indians. After Osho's passing, Western disciples and Indian authorities struggled for control over his work and the commune's management.

The establishment of "The Inner Circle" by Osho and the appointment of key individuals such as Sw. Anand Jayesh and Amrito brought about significant friction. Some of Osho's Indian followers felt that the Western disciples, particularly Jayesh and Amrito, had gained undue control over the decision-making processes and the direction of Osho's legacy.

On the other hand, the Western disciples argued that Osho had personally chosen them to carry forward his work and vision. They highlighted Osho's words about leaving his dream to Jayesh, indicating that he had entrusted the Western followers with preserving and expanding his teachings and the commune.

This clash of perspectives, cultural differences, and power struggles have led to prolonged and complex legal battles over the control and management of Osho's work and assets (most notably his intellectual property and the Puna ashram). The controversy over the control of Osho's legacy between Westerners and Indians continues to be a significant and sensitive issue within the Osho community and has made frequent news in India.

As recently as this decade, a court battle ensued over Osho International Foundation's (OIF) proposal to sell some of the Ashram's land. In Fall 2023, India's Joint Charity Commission rejected the application and ordered a forensic audit of the Ashram's finances.

The Indian popular press has dubbed the group fighting current OIF leadership the "Osho rebel group." This group points to changes in how the ashram has been run over the years, which they perceive as damaging Osho's spiritual legacy and distancing the movement from the personality of its founder. OIF discontinued the initiation into sannyasa and prohibited the wearing of malas at the ashram. The latter prohibition had the effect of essentially barring Indian followers from the ashram grounds.

In March 2023, around 1,000 protestors convened outside the ashram to express their discontent with OIF's management and against the prohibition on wearing malas inside the "resort."

Osho's Indian followers continue to promote his teachings and carry on the neo-sannyas movement as Osho had during his lifetime. Longtime sannyasin Swami Anand Arun has been a critical figure in this movement. His ashram, Osho Tapoban, is located in the serene hills of Nepal and serves as a center for meditation, personal growth, and exploring Osho's teachings. Established in the early 1990s, the ashram allows individuals to engage in various meditation practices, workshops, and retreats. The ashram's environment is designed to foster a sense of peace and introspection, aligning with Osho's emphasis on mindfulness and self-discovery. The ashram offers a range of programs, including meditation sessions, therapy groups, and spiritual discourses, all intended to help individuals explore their inner selves and connect with the core principles of Osho's teachings. Interestingly, the practices conducted at the ashram include the ceremony of *arati*, a traditional Hindu ritual that involves offering light from wicks soaked in ghee or oil.

Approximately 30 miles south of Delhi is Osho Dham. The meditation center was founded by Swami Om Prakash Saraswatiover two decades ago. Osho Dham publishes a Hindi-language magazine devoted to Osho's teachings. Their website offers a free archive of discourse recordings in both Hindi and English.

Rajneeshpuram
A Bibliography

Osho's books (based on discourses, meetings with disciples, and letters) comprise approximately 250 original titles in Hindi and around 280 original titles in English. His books have been published in 58 languages. Currently, the Sannyas Wiki lists more than 4,700 titles in 32 languages. Additionally, over the years newspapers and magazines dedicated to Osho were published in over 50 countries. Numerous "compilation" books, containign selected material on specific topics, continue to be published by St. Martin's Publishing Group a division of Macmillan one of the "big five" publishing houses.

The following is compiled from my personal collection, with additional information from "The Lao Tzu Book List," an extract from the Osho Lao Tzu Library of English language books dated 1 November 1992. This listing comprises books produced by the publishing operation at the Ranch. Unlike the editions from the previous decade produced at the Pune ashram which were predominantly comprised of hardcovers, the books produced at the ranch were primarly less expensive mass market paperbacks. During the early 1980s, it was not uncomon to find select titles in mass market chain bookstores in American malls. My first Rajneesh titles were purchased at the B. Dalton in the Bangor Mall. After the closure of the commune, publication operations initially relocated to Boulder, Colorado.

PUBLICATION MARKS

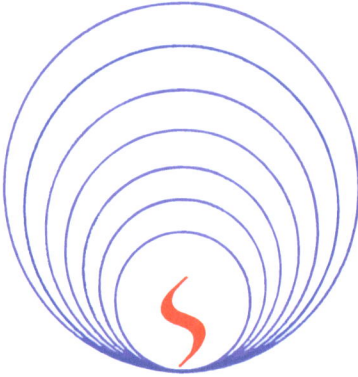

Jivan Jagruti Kendrawas trust established in 1969. Flame logo used until 1974.

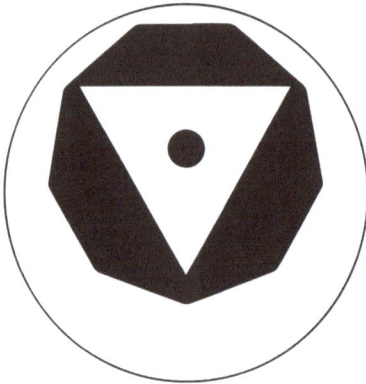

Renamed Neo Sannyas Foundation in 1974 with the opening of the Pune Ashram, also known as the Rejneesh Foundation. Used on all in-house publications during the Pune I period.

Two bird logo put into place when the Chidvilas Rajneesh Meditation Center in Montclair, New Jersey became the Rajneesh Foundation International with the puchase of the Big Muddy Ranch. Used on all in-house publications 1981-1985.

Ah, This! Responses to Disciples' and Visitors' Questions and Zen Stories, December 1982 (7.000 copies) Talkes delivered January 1980 Pune, India.

And Now, And Here, Vol 1: Discourses from the Meditation Camp at Dwarka, Gujarat, India, July 1984 (10,000 copies) Talks in Bombay 1969-1970 Talks delivered October 1969 Dwarka meditation camp

And Now, And Here, Vol 2, India, July 1985 (First printing 10,000)

A Cup of Tea, December 1983 (First printing 10,000) Letters to disciples 1962-1971

Beware of Socialism, June 1984 (First printing 10,000) Talks given April 1970, Cross Maidan, Bombay.

The Book: Series I from A to H: An Introduction to the Teachings of Bhagwan Shree Rajneesh, March 1984 (10,000 copies). Collection of quotes arranged alphabetically by subject. Authorship of the three books in this series was originally credited to Bhagwan Shree Rajneesh. Following his repudiation of Rajneeshism, he revoked the attribution of authorship.

The Book: Series II from I to Q: An Introduction to the Teachings of Bhagwan Shree Rajneesh, March 1984 (10,000 copies).

The Book: Series III from R to Z: An Introduction to the Teachings of Bhagwan Shree Rajneesh, March 1984 (10,000 copies).

The Book of Books: Discourses on The Dhammapada of Gautam the Buddha, Vol. 1, July 1982 (5,000 copies) Talks given June 1979 Buddha Hall, Pune, India.

The Book of Books: Discourses on The Dhammapada of Gautam the Buddha, Vol. 2, December 1983 (10,000 copies) Talks given July 1979 Buddha Hall, Pune, India.

The Book of Books: Discourses on The Dhammapada of Gautam the Buddha, Vol. 3, December 1984 (10,000 copies) Talks given August 1979 Buddha Hall, Pune, India.

The Book of Books: Discourses on The Dhammapada of Gautam the Buddha, Vol. 4, July 1985 (10,000 copies) Talks given August 1979 Buddha Hall, Pune, India.

The Book of the Secrets: Discourses on Vigyana Bhairava Tantra, Vol 4, Second edition 1982 (40,000 copies) Talks given May, June, July 1973, Woodlands, Bombay, India.

The Book of the Secrets: Discourses on Vigyana Bhairava Tantra, Vol 5, Second edition March 1984 (10,000 copies) Talks given July, August, November 1973, Woodlands, Bombay, India.

Books I Have Loved, July 1985 (10,000 copies) Extremporainous talks November - December 1981, Lao Tzu Grove, Rajneeshpuram.

The Book of Wisdom: Discourses on Atisha's Seven Points of Mind Training, Vol 1, March 1983 (7,000 copies) Talks given February and March 1979, Buddha Hall, Pune, India.

The Book of Wisdom: Discourses on Atisha's Seven Points of Mind Training, Vol 2, September 1984 (10,000 copies) Talks given February 1979, Buddha Hall, Pune, India.

Don't Bite My Finger, Look Where I'm Pointing, December 1982 (First printing 3,000) Initiation talks, Pune, India March 1978.

Don't Let Yourself Be Upset by the Sutra, rather Upset the Sutra Yourself, July 1985 (First printing 5,000) Darshan diary, Pune, India August-September 1979

Don't Look Before You Leap, March 1983 (First printing 10,000) Initiation talks Pune, India July 1978.

Glimpses of a Golden Childhood, September 1985 (First printing 10,000) Extemporanoius talks at Lao Tzu House, Rajneeshpuram circ 1981-1982.

God's Got a Thing About You, July 1983 (First printing 10,000) Initiation talks Pune, India September 1978.

The Goose is Out, July 1982 (10,000 copies) Responses to disciples questions March 1982, Buddha Hall, Pune, India.

The Guest: Talks on Kabir, December 1981 (5,000 copies) Talks given April-May 1979, Buddha Hall, Pune, India.

Guida Spirituale: Discourses on the Desiderata, March 1983 (First printing 10,000) Talks given August-September 1980, Buddha Hall, Pune, India.

Hsin Hsin Ming: The Book of Nothing: Discourses on the Faith Mind of Sosan, 1983 (Second edition 10,000) Talks given October 1974, Lao Tzu balcony, Pune, India.

I Am That: Discourses on the Isa Upanishad, July 1984 (First printing 10,000) Talks given October 1980, Buddha Hall, Pune, India.

I Say unto You, Vol 1: Talks on the Sayings of Jesus, Second edition July 1983 (10,000 copies) Talks given October-November 1977, Buddha Hall, Pune, India.

In Search of the Miraculous, September 1984 (10,000 copies) Translated from Hindi talks given May-July 1970 Nargol meditation camp and Bombay.

Just Around the Corner: Initiation Talks Between Master and Desciple, January 1984.

Krishna: The Man and His Philosophy, July 1985 (10,000 copies) Translated from Hindi talks given July-October 1970 Bombay and Manali meditation camp.

The Last Testament, Vol. 1: Interviews with the World Press, June 1986 (10,000 copies). Published by Rajneesh Publications, Boulder, Colorado, after relocation from the Ranch.

The Long and the Short and the All: Excerpts from early discourses and letters, July 1984 (10,000 copies).

The Mustard Seed: Discourses on the Sayings of Jesus from the Gospel According to Thomas, December 1984 (10,000 copies) Talks given August-September 1974, Lao Tzu balcony, Pune, India.

No Water, No Moon, September 1984 (10,000 copies) talks given August 1974 Lao Tzu balcony, Pune, India.

Notes of a Madman, September 1985 (10,000 copies) Extemporaneous talks at Lao Tzu Grove, Rahneeshpuram.

The Orange Book: The Meditation Techniques of Bhagwan Shree Rajneesh, Second edition January 1983 (50,000 copies) compilation.

The Perfect Way: Discourse given by Bhagwan Shree Rajneesh at HIs first medication camp held in Rajasthan, India July 1984 (First printing 10,000) Talks given June 1964 Shri Muchala Mahavira, Ranakpur, meditation camp.

Philosophia Perennis, Vol 1: Speaking on the Golden Verses of Pythagoras, December 1981 (5,000 copies)Talks given December 1978, Buddha Hall, Pune, India.

Philosophia Perennis, Vol 2: Speaking on the Golden Verses of Pythagoras, December 1981 (5,000 copies) Talks given December 1978 - January 1979, Buddha Hall, Pune,

India.

Philosophia Ultima: Discourses on the Mandukya Upanishad, December 1983 (10,000 copies) Talks given December 1980, Buddha Hall, Pune, India.

The Rainbow Bridge, March 1985 (5,000 copies) Initiation talks July 1979, Chuang Tzu Auditorium, Pune, India.

Rajneeshism: An Introduction to Bhagwan Shree Rajneesh and His Religion, July 1983 (10,000 copies), revised second edition November 1983 (10,000 copies).

The Rajneesh Bible, Vol. 1, March 1985 (10,000 copies) Talks given October-November 1984, Lao Tzu Grove, Rajneeshpuram.

The Rajneesh Bible, Vol. 2, June 1985 (10,000 copies) Talks given November-December 1984, Lao Tzu Grove, Rajneeshpuram.

The Rajneesh Bible, Vol. 3, September 1985 (10,000 copies) Talks given December-January 1984, Lao Tzu Grove, Rajneeshpuram.

Rajneesh Neo-Tarot (deck) January 1984.

The Rajneesh Upanishad, November 1986, Boulder, Colorado (5,000 copies) Talks given to the Rajneesh International University of Mysticism.

The Sacred Yes, September 1983 (10,000 copies) Initiation talks November 1978, Chuang Tzu Auditorium, Pune, India.

The Secret of the Secrets: Talks on the Secret of the Golden Flower, Vol 1, Second edition July 1982 (5,000 copies) Talks given May, August-September 1978, Buddha Hall, Pune, India.

The Secret of the Secrets: Talks on the Secret of the Golden Flower,

Vol 2, Second edition September 1983 (10,000 copies) Talks given May, August 1978, Buddha Hall, Pune, India.

The Shadow of the Bamboo, July 1984 (10,000 copies) Initiation talks April 1979, Chuang Tzu auditorium, Pune, India.

Snap Your Fingers, Slap Your Face and Wake Up! December 1984 (5,000 copies) Initiation talks June 1979 Chuang Tzu Auditorium, Pune, India.

Tantra, Spirituality & Sex, September 1983 (First printing 40,000) Compilation.

Tantra: The Supreme Understanding: Discourses on the Tantric Way of Tilopa's Song of Mahamudra, Second edition July 1984 (10,000 copies) Talks given February 1975 Chuang Tzu Auditorium, Pune, India.

Tao: The Golden Gate, Vol 1: Discourses on Ko Hsuan's The Classic of Purity, March 1984 (10,000 copies) Talks given June 1980 Buddha Hall, Pune, India.

Tao: The Golden Gate, Vol 2: Discourses on Ko Hsuan's The Classic of Purity, March 1985 (10,000 copies) Talks given June 1980 Buddha Hall, Pune, India.

Tao: The Three Treasures, Vol 1: Talks on Fragments from Tao Te Ching by Lao Tzu, Second edition July 1983 (10,000 copies) Talks June 1975 Chuang Tzu Auditorium, Pune, India.

Theologia Mystica: Discourses on the Treatise of St. Dionysius, July 1983 (10,000 copies) Talks delivered August 1980, Buddha Hall, Pune, India.

This Very Body the Buddha This Very Place the Lotus Paradise: A photo-biography of Bhagwan Shree Rajneesh and His work 1978-1984, December 1984, (limited edition of 1,500 copies).

Walking in Zen, Sitting in Zen: Responses to Disciples' and Visitors' Questions and Zen Stories, December 1982 (7,000 copies), March 1980, Buddha Hall, Pune, India.

The Wild Geese and the Water, July 1985 (10,000 copies) Responses to Questions from Disciples and Visitors, February 1981, Buddha Hall, Pune, India.

Won't You Join the Dance? Initiation Talks between Master and Disciples, December 1983, February 1979, Chuang Tzu Auditorium, Pune, India.

Yoga: The Science of the Soul, Vol 1, July 1984 (10,000 copies), December 1973 - January 1974.

Yoga: The Science of the Soul, Vol 2, July 1984 (10,000 copies), January 1974.

Yoga: The Science of the Soul, Vol 3, July 1984 (10,000 copies), March 1974.

You Ain't Seen Nothin' Yet: Initiation Talks between Master and Disciple, March 1984 (10,000 copies) March 1979, Chuang Tzu Auditorium, Pune, India.

Zen: The Special Transmission, December 1984 (10,000 copies) Talks given July 1980, Buddha Hall, Pune, India.

Zorba the Buddha Rajneesh Cookbook, July 1984 (10,000 copies).

Bibliography

The following books were used in the preparation of this book:

Bauman, Zygmunt. *Modernity and the Holocaust*. Cornell University: Ithaca, NY, 1989.

Brecher, Max. *A Passage to America*. Book Quest, Bombay, 1993.

Carter, Lewis F. *Charisma and Control in Rajneeshpuram: The Role of Shared Values In the Creation of a Community*. Cambridge University: Cambridge, 1990.

Fabijan DJ, Morris R, Murray GM. "The effect of nitrous oxide on hearing." *Anaesth Intensive Care*, vol. 28, no. 3, June 2000, pp. 270-5.

Fitzgerald, Frances. *Cities On a Hill*. Simon & Schuster: New York, 1987.

Franklin, Satya Bharti. *The Promise of Paradise*. Station Hill: New York, 1992.

Garakani, A., Jaffe, R.J., Savla, D., Welch, A.K., Protin, C.A., Bryson, E.O. and McDowell, D.M. (2016), "Neurologic, psychiatric, and other medical manifestations of nitrous oxide abuse: A systematic review of the case literature." *Am J Addict*, vol. 25, 2016, pp. 358-369.

Hamilton, Rosemary. *Hellbent For Enlightenment: Unmasking Sex, Power, and Death with a Notorious Master*. White Cloud Press: Ashland, OR, 1998.

Haney, Craig, Curtis Banks & Philip Zimbardo. "Interpersonal

Dynamics in a Simulated Prison," *International Journal of Criminology and Penology* vol. VI. (1968), pp. 69-97. Cited in Bauman.

Jenkins, Philip. *Mystics & Messiahs: Cults and New Religions in American History*. Oxford University: Oxford, 2001.

Joshi, Vasant. *The Awakened One: The Life and Work of Bhagwan Shree Rajneesh*. Harper & Row: New York, 1982.

Milgram, Stanley. *Obedience to Authority: An Experimental View*. Tavistock: London, 1974.

Nabben, Jan van Amsterdam, Ton Nabben, Wim van den Brink. "Recreational nitrous oxide use: Prevalence and risks." *Regulatory Toxicology and Pharmacology*, vol. 73, no. 3, December 2015, pp. 790-796.

Rajneesh, Bhagwan Shree (Osho). *Beyond Psychology: Talks in Uruguay*. Osho Media International, 2008.

_____. *Krishna: The Man and His Philosophy*. Rajneesh Foundation International: Rajneeshpuram, OR, 1985.

_____. *The Last Testament: Interviews with the World Press, volume I*. Rajneesh Publications, Inc.: Boulder, CO, 1986.

_____. *The Last Testament, volume IV*.

_____. *The Perfect Way*. Motilal Babarsidass: Delhi, 1993.

Sethi, N.K., Mullin, P., Torgovnick, J. et al. "Nitrous oxide 'Whippit' abuse presenting with cobalamin responsive psychosis." *J. Med. Toxicol.*, vol. 2, 2006, pp. 71–74

Sheela, Anand. *Don't Kill Him! The story of my life with Bhagwan Rajneesh*. FingerPrint! Delhi, 2012.

Shunyo, Prem. *Diamond Days With Osho*. Motilal Banarsidass: Delhi, 1993.

Tsung-Ta Chiang, Chih-Tsung Hung, Wei-Ming Wang,

Jiunn-Tay Lee, Fu-Chi Yang. "Recreational Nitrous Oxide Abuse-Induced Vitamin B12 Deficiency in a Patient Presenting with Hyperpigmentation of the Skin." *Case Rep Dermatol*, 1 August 2013.